INTRODUCTION
Foreword from John

At 12 noon on June 3rd, 2006, I quit my job working as a human-robot in a car plant and have been full time running my own online business ever since.

Since then, I have become a top 1% Platinum ClickBank Seller whose digital products have netted me $5+ million in sales on the ClickBank platform alone. I have also reached the top 1% status as a seller and as an affiliate on JVZoo and have personally generated well over $10 million in sales.

Since 2008, I've helped over 3,000 entrepreneurs start (or grow) their online businesses. And to date, my students have generated more than $23 million in profits as a direct result of following my step-by-step programs.

These days, I specialize in helping freedom-focused individuals create, launch and sell their first digital product online, even if they don't consider themself to be an expert and have no idea where to start.

This book will serve 2 purposes.

Firstly, I will cover all that I know about Internet Marketing and digital product creation, plus what I have learned on this crazy journey so far. Once you have read this book you will discover literally everything you need to know, to build a 6 figure per year online business from your own digital products.

John Thornhill

Secondly, I am hoping that after reading this book you will see exactly how I operate online with my honest and ethical approach, and in turn will then want to work with me and want to discover how I can help you get to 6 figures per year as fast as humanly possible, and in most cases put you on that journey in under 60 days.

I am going to say one more thing before we begin, most people who read this book will do absolutely nothing with the info presented and that's just the way it is. Over the years I have learned that a lot of people live a life of entitlement and play the blame game for their failure and unfortunately there's nothing that can be done to change that.

Hopefully, you are not like most people and will do something with the info presented, just remember that if you ever have any questions or need any help, I am here to support you via the link above.

So, with that out of the way let's get started…

CONTENTS

John Thornhill

PROOF THIS SYSTEM WORKS

What I'm about to share with you in this book is the exact system, that at the time of writing, myself and my students have used to generate total profits of over twenty-three million dollars.

And no, that's not a typo. This system is the backbone of my 7-figure online business and I'm going to share it all with you.

Over the past few years, I've taught this process to my students and the results have been incredible! Just check out some of these earnings from a handful of my students that can all be verified. (I'll share more success stories later)

Omar Martin, $7,000,000…

Steven Alvey, $1,000,000…

Randy Smith, $1,000,000…

Shelley Penney, $320,000…

Dawud Islam, $100,000…

Eric Hammer, $250,000

And the success stories just keep on coming!

These are real, everyday people that are getting life-changing results. And the people who have built these businesses come from all walks of life and from all corners of the globe…

Plus, many of the students you will hear about today started this when they had a 9-5 job and they began this journey this as a side income…

Now, of course, many of the people who have gone through this system have since quit their day jobs to focus on this. In fact, all the names you see above are now full time online.

But we have other students who've chosen to keep their 9-5 jobs because they like that lifestyle, and they can run this business in just 3-4 hours per week.

So, it doesn't matter who you are, it doesn't matter where you're from, and it doesn't matter what language you speak…

Literally, anyone can make this work and it's up to you how far you want to take it.

"Dedicating myself to actually following through was my single biggest achievement"

- Nick Woodman - CEO GoPro

THE BILLION DOLLAR OPPORTUNITY

Let me ask you a couple of things.

True or false?

At some point in the past, you have paid for a digital product that was not essential to your survival?

Not necessarily from me, but you've paid for something out there online that is not essential to you surviving day-to-day.

Maybe it was an eBook or Kindle book, maybe it was an online course, or maybe it was some sort of software or audiobook.

I already know the answer is true, after all, you paid for this book :-)

But seriously, I bet that there is a ton of other stuff you've bought online that wasn't necessary for your survival.

Now… is there anything wrong with that?

No, of course not. It's a good thing.

You paid for them because they added value to your life.

So, that one was an easy one…

Now, what about this one.

True or false?

There are millions of people out there right now who would pay you at least $27 if you just put the right thing in front of them?

What do you think, true or false?

Well, let me tell you that there are millions of folks out there who would just love to give you their $27 if you just provided the right kind of value to them.

What do you think?

I'm hoping you're saying true and already starting to see where we are going with this.

Okay, one more…

True or false?

Most people never generate consistent income online because they don't have an asset of their own to sell?

What do you think?

John Thornhill

Here's the thing…

I love selling products on Amazon…

I love selling products on eBay…

I love dropshipping…

And I love affiliate marketing…

In fact, at the time of writing this I just received $13,000 from promoting someone else's product as an affiliate. I promoted their webinar to the subscribers on my mailing list (more on this later) and we generated $26,000 in sales and I received 50% in commissions, not bad for sending a handful of emails.

So, I love all those things, but the problem is… I'm at the mercy of their business in some of those things.

That means if Amazon or eBay changed the rules tomorrow, then a lot of people would go out of business.

However, having an asset of your own, that makes you money month after month where you control most of the process, that's huge and no one can take that away from you as it's your product selling from your website

Now, let me ask you, why do most people not have a product or service of their own for sale online?

You could argue it's a symptom of not being able to focus or a lack of confidence. Or maybe it's a symptom of "shiny object syndrome" and buying product after product or course after course and doing nothing with it. (Remember I said most people will do nothing with the information in this book?)

But really, in the grand scheme of things, it's not having that digital asset of your own that's a big deal and it's something you need to address and that's what we will do in this book.

What you must understand is, right now we're living in one of the most exciting times in history, but we're also living in a time of great financial uncertainty.

Just turn on the news for five minutes and you will be convinced that the world is going to come to an end.

In 2020, more than 40 million Americans filed for unemployment.

And a further 63% of US workers were living paycheck-to-paycheck.

The COVID-19 pandemic forced massive changes around the world, and the biggest thing that had to change is our job market.

Having a job and being an employee used to provide financial security for people.

John Thornhill

You work for a big company, you stay there, retire with a nice pension; everything works out, but now people laugh when they hear the term "job security," because there's basically no such thing anymore.

There was a recent report in Time magazine, that explained how millions of Americans lost their jobs in the pandemic.

And it gets worse, as the report explained why robots and artificial intelligence (or AI for short) are replacing humans faster than ever.

In fact, it's predicted that robots could replace an estimated 20 million jobs within the next decade... Scary stuff!

And I don't want to pile on the misery too much, but Elon Musk, the CEO of Tesla, recently predicted in an interview that robots will be able to do everything better than us.

"Robots will be able to do everything better than us. I have exposure to the most cutting-edge AI, and I think people should be really concerned by it".
- Elon Musk - CEO Tesla

But the question is, what does all of this mean for the future?

Well, many economic experts predict that the after-effects of the pandemic will continue to create massive changes around the world.

This means two things:

Firstly, if you don't own (or work for) a business that makes most of its money selling online, you're in a vulnerable position.

And secondly, if you don't control your own income, your livelihood will always be at the mercy of someone else.

That's the bad news. Here's the good news...

Right now, there's a never been a better opportunity to build your own online business and set yourself free for life...

That's because owning your own business is by far the best way to protect yourself from economic changes.

You can't be fired or laid off because you own the business!

This means that it doesn't matter what happens with the economy in the coming months as successful business owners will likely continue to get wealthier because they are captains of their own ship.

John Thornhill

They control their own destinies because they run their own businesses.

Peter Drucker, one of the most successful businesspeople of all time, said that universities won't survive.

The future is outside the traditional campus, outside the traditional classroom. Distance learning is coming on fast, and so far, his prediction is starting to come true.

What Peter Drucker calls distance learning is one of the fastest-growing industries today.

But we don't call it distance learning...

We call it eLearning.

People are learning online, through digital products, and when you look around today, you'll notice three things:

The first thing is that everyone is reading, they're watching videos, and they're reading and listening to information they search for, find, and often buy online...

The second thing is that the amount of time they invest doing this is growing because technology allows them to consume content on more devices than ever such as their phones and tablets as well as their computers.

And the third thing is that the amount of money they invest doing it is also growing.

People all over the world are turning to online education to learn new things about every topic imaginable, and this has created a massive demand for digital teaching products...

Which is what we're talking about here in this book...

Things like eBooks, online video courses, audio programs, membership websites, software, WordPress plugins, and a lot more.

And this trend is only going to continue in the coming months and years.

John Thornhill

THE JOURNEY STARTS (OR ENDS) HERE

I have already said twice now that most people will do absolutely nothing with the information presented in this book, however the fact you are still reading means you have made it further than some people as I know for a fact some people will buy this book and not even read the first page.

The thing is, I'm as guilty as most people for not seeing things through. I have a ton of books I've bought with good intentions that I have not read yet. Although they do look good on my bookshelf. And I have invested in a ton of keep fit equipment over the years that never gets used and let's not even get started on some of the kitchen appliances that I have bought (George Foreman grill, anyone?) that are sitting in the cupboards gathering dust. So, if you can relate to this then you're not alone.

However, as I said earlier, after being in this business full time since 2006 and coaching people since 2008, I have noticed most people simply look for excuses for their failure and until that changes, they will never become a success online. In this chapter I am going to list the reasons people fail and the excuses they make and after reading this you will be able to decide if you want to continue this journey and make it to chapter 4.

Mindset!

First, I want to talk about mindset…

If you have the wrong mindset you are doomed to fail right from the start. The truth is most successful marketers all have one thing in common, they have a positive mindset. They believe they will become successful eventually no matter how long it takes.

If you go online full of negativity, doubts, and very little self-belief then it is inevitable that failure will come very easy for you. So right from the start you must believe in yourself and keep believing in yourself no matter how long it takes to become successful, whether it's a matter of weeks, months, or even years. Believe in yourself, be positive and it will happen.

"Whether you think you can or you think you can't, you're right".

- Henry Ford

Technical ability!

Having a lack of technical ability is probably one of the biggest excuses I see people make online for their failure, yes, I did say excuse as that all it is.

Let me tell you, 'it's too technical for me' should not be part of your vocabulary if you want to become successful online. Do you know what I do when I find something too technical? I simply go to Google or YouTube and find out how to do it, simple as that.

Want to learn FTP? Simply search for 'how to ftp'
Want to learn how to install a WordPress blog? Search for 'how to install a WordPress blog'

See how easy that is? So next time you tell yourself you can't do something let me tell you that you can. You have the most advanced educational tool at your fingertips, it's called the Internet, never forget that.

Plus, if something was mega technical you can outsource it and get someone else to do it. Some stuff I do online is way beyond my technical abilities, but I have access to a programmer who can take care of that for me.

Also, think about this for a moment, millions of people are searching online every single day for solutions to their problems and that's where you and I come in. We find out what problems people are facing and come up with the solutions in our digital products.

Lazy!

Another reason people are failing, especially when starting out is they are just too damn lazy (there, I said it) and want to do absolutely nothing with their lives and somehow generate an income online.

We all wish we could plant dollar bills and grow an unlimited amount of money while sitting back doing nothing. All I will say is good luck with that money plant.

This is one of the biggest reasons people fail. They see promises of easy riches for doing very little work at all, when the truth is there are no easy way to make money online.

That's why clever copywriters paint the picture of easy riches for doing very little work, they do this because it appeals to a lot of people who simply don't want to do any work and believe me there are a lot of people like this out there.

I've seen first-hand how people simply don't want to put the work in, I've watched them fail to follow simple instructions that I've given them because it involves a little bit of work.

Believe me, no matter what anyone tells you, if you want to succeed in this business, you better be prepared to put the work in, and lots of it.

However, when you do put the work in further down the line, you can reap the rewards as you learn to automate your business and have it work for you. That's the point when you can be sitting on a tropical beach sipping on a Pina Colada while your busines runs on autopilot.

Herd mentality!

There are two types of marketers online, there's the herd and then there's the people who sell to the herd.

The herd will buy just about everything that's put out there, especially the big product launches. They will act upon scarcity, urgency, controversy, rave reviews and so on. They will follow everyone else, especially when taking part in online social media discussions. They will also buy into the dream, whether this is to lose weight, improve their life or make more money online. This is called herd mentality and to be truly successful you need to separate yourself from the herd and start *selling* to the herd.

You need to be the one creating products and services that the herd will invest into; you need to be the one creating urgency and scarcity. Once you can truly separate yourself from the herd and 'get it' you will start to see success.

Now, I do want to say that I still act like part of the herd sometimes. I can still be 'sold to' just like anyone else, but the trick is to spot when you're being 'sold to' and learn from it.

Quitting is not an option!

If you encounter a problem and give up, you will fail. I don't really need to say much more here, do I? If you give up each time you hit a roadblock then tasks won't be complete, products won't get finished and brought to the market and all your time and effort will be wasted. Remember what I said earlier about using Google and YouTube to learn how to accomplish technical tasks?

I see each problem I face as a challenge. Some days I seem to have no issues at all and other days the problems just seem to pile up and I'd be lying if I said it doesn't sometimes stress me out. However, no matter how big the roadblock is I never ever give up and eventually always find a solution. It's this Mindset that has enabled me to generate millions of dollars in sales. So never ever give up, ever, and if you do get stressed from time to time remember it's normal.

"I have not failed. I've just found 10,000 ways that won't work."
- Thomas A. Edison

Negativity!

I may get some flak for this, but it needs to be said. So, you hate your job, or even worse you've lost your job, or maybe you've recently been divorced, or you are up to your eyes in debt, or you are in some other situation where your luck is down. When this happens, you can do one of two things. You can be negative and moan about your situation or get down to business and put the situation right.

I was in a ton of debt before I started to see success online, I had a job that I hated and I used to live from month to month. Guess what I did? Well for starters I didn't moan about my situation and I got down to business. Sure, it took a couple of years to see any results, but I never gave up (mindset) and I kept at it. This is what you need to do if you find yourself in a situation you don't like.

In fact, many successful online marketers usually hit a massive low before they really get down to business. Something happens in their life that makes them so angry they change their mindset and become determined to turn things around. Remember when you hit rock bottom the only way is up from that point.

However, some constantly go through life thinking that it's someone else's fault they are in their current situation. They constantly moan about having to commute to a job they hate, and they blame others (the world) for their situation.

Let me tell you something, the world owes you nothing. In fact, there is only one person who can change your situation, it's not me, not the lottery board, (I wish) not your boss that you may hate, or your president or prime minister. It's you... never forget that.

If you can relate to this and hate your current situation, get angry, change your mindset, and get to work to put it right.

No time!

Weirdly, even though technology has made our lives much easier (take email over regular mail for example) everyone seems to have less time.

"I could never have an online business that can be successful as I work 12 hours a day, have to go home and look after the kids, have to do the shopping, cleaning, ironing, wash the car, cut the grass"

I see this sort of excuse time and time again and I'm going to be honest here it boils my blood and if someone said they had no time this would be my answer...

So, you really have no time? Let me ask you if you have a TV or a games console, or if you spend time on sites such as Twitter or Facebook, or if you're constantly browsing the Internet looking at nothing in particular?

Well take an hour or so a day from that stuff and work at building your business. Turn the TV off, stay off your phone, stop browsing the internet and get some real work done, the latest box set can wait, after all it's all on demand these days.

Lack of funds!

This is another big excuse I see people make but I want to make sure I don't say the wrong things here. Obviously if you are in a situation where you are struggling to put food on the table then you have a perfectly valid excuse to say money is an issue. However, it needn't be. You see if you don't have any money, you do have something else that can work in your favour and that is time. That is if you don't make the excuse of having none.

Most digital products can be created 100% free; all you need is some hosting and a domain name to get started, and I'm sure no matter what your situation is you can afford it; you can grab a domain for a few dollars and hosting can be bought for around $10 per month. And even if you can't afford that, some marketplaces will even host everything for you. So, you really don't have to let lack of funding hold you back.

After all it's not costing me anything to sit down and write this book, is it? I am writing this book with Google Docs which is 100% free. So, it needn't cost you anything to work on your project.

THE HAMSTER WHEEL OF FAILURE MOST MARKETERS FACE

Does this sound like you?
"I have tried many different types of business but have yet to succeed. I need a low cost very easy (broken way down, step by baby step) way to see some success so that I feel I can accomplish what others have done. A lot of Internet Marketers assume too much and skip over some of the very basic steps to succeed online."

Or could this be you?
"It's great to tell people how to succeed. There is no shortage of that type of product out there. However, showing someone how to succeed is much more important... I personally consider myself to be a bright person, but much of this info - marketing info products - is overwhelming. I need a step-by-step guide to the entire process."

Or maybe you can relate to this?
"I'm tired of everyone promising they can make me a millionaire. I want to work at this and make it happen. I'm an honest person and don't want to lie or cheat to make money. I know there's got to be some honest people left in this world."

John Thornhill

Or what about this?
"John, I feel so brain dead and up against a wall with this stuff. You would be my hero of all time if you could somehow cause me to see through all this maze of stuff and make serious sense of it all to where I can just take off and do it with confidence."

Just so you know, those comments aren't made up, they were left by my subscribers when I ran a recent survey. I could probably give you hundreds or maybe even thousands of similar comments if I go through my emails over the last 10 years.

This leads me on to something I want to briefly talk to you about that I call **"The Internet Marketing Black Hole."**

You see, I got my start online way back in 2002.

And back then, there wasn't as many marketers' lists or products being pushed on you.

But if I was to start over again from scratch, I think it would be a lot harder for me to stay focused.

You see, the big difference between then and now is that there's so much "noise" in the marketplace today.

That's why I believe so many people fall into this vicious cycle where they…

1. Buy a new product…

2. Give it 1-2 weeks of effort…
3. Get stuck and lose motivation…
4. Get distracted by a new shiny object…
5. Give up and start all over again…

And this is a huge problem!

Because so for as long as you remain chained to this cycle, you'll never stick at anything long enough to see results.

And I know this sounds cliché, but the truth is, it's not your fault.

Today, there are so many shiny objects being dangled in front of you that it's impossible not to get sucked in…

Which is exactly what the greedy marketing gurus want!

Therefore, I'm a big believer in taking no notice of the latest launches that happen every single day promising untold riches for clicking your mouse a few times…

Because, for most people, all these launches are just shiny objects that will keep you distracted and chained to this cycle, and if you find yourself in this situation you need to stop as you are doing yourself more harm than good and are simply wasting time and money.

John Thornhill

So, the question for you now becomes...
"What makes this book different from any other training I've looked at in the past?"

Well...

First, when you follow my instructions and create your own digital product, you're building a long-term asset instead of chasing short-term cash flow...

Second, it's not based on a fad, gimmick, or loophole, because we don't want to waste our time and money building something that might be here today, but gone tomorrow...

Third, you'll be building a real, legitimate business that you can be proud of. Chances are, if you're anything like most of the people who become my students, you're sick and tired of all the automated "get rich quick" type stuff that we see peddled every single day.

Fourth, you're not competing against 1,000s of other people who are all promoting the same products. If you've ever tried affiliate marketing, you already know what I mean. The competition is huge, and we will cover that later...

Fifth, with this business, you do the work once, then get paid over and over again. So, you won't be trading your time for money. This is a true set-and-forget type strategy...

Always be willing to help!

Yes, I emboldened that line above as I want to make sure you understand this.

I know for a fact a reason for a lot of my success is due to the fact I am willing to help others as much as I possibly can. If you contact my helpdesk or send me a personal email you will always get a response from me whether you are a customer of mine or not. I do my very best to help every single person that contacts me no matter what the problem is. I provide help for free, and I take pride in the fact that no email or support ticket goes ignored. You can test this out by going to johnthornhill.com/more and contacting me. (Go on, try it)

Now what do you think that has done for my reputation?

Well, let me tell you it's done a great deal, in fact if you Google my name, then apart from finding the other John Thornhill's, one who works for The Financial Times and one who is a professional wrestler, you will find yours truly, and you will probably find 99.9% of the stuff you find out about me is positive, and that's the way I want it to stay, so I will continue to look after my subscribers and customers.

It's very important you get what I'm trying to tell you here, so many people simply chase the money when they should be concentrating on helping others, do that and the money will come in all on its own.

THE VENDOR VERSUS THE AFFILIATE

Most beginners are taught to do affiliate marketing because on the surface, it looks like the easiest thing to do, you just promote a product and collect the commissions without having to worry about product creation or things like customer support.

However, let me explain why affiliate marketing is not what you think it is, especially when starting out.

Just in case you need a refresher, affiliate marketing is where you act as the "middleman" and get paid a commission every time you sell someone else's product. The beauty of affiliate marketing in the digital age is you can get paid very high commissions as there are no physical products involved. Obviously when you promote a physical product there are extra costs involved so commissions can be very low. In fact, some of Amazon's commission rates are as low as 1% while some product vendors will pay 100% commissions to promote their digital offer.

So, you can see the appeal of becoming an affiliate for digital products.

But here's the thing…

The core idea behind affiliate marketing is simple, but it doesn't work, and I'll give you a real-world example.

There is a product of mine called Simple Traffic Solutions (Google it) that teaches people all about driving free traffic to their websites. I pay 100% commissions to affiliates who promote this because I have a very profitable sales funnel that rewards me on backend sales so can afford to do this. It is a very attractive offer for affiliates and lots of affiliates promote it.

Now, let's imagine that you are an affiliate for this offer.

You send me traffic, and every time you make a sale, I send you a commission. This is very, very simple to understand as I'm sure you'll agree.

But as I said a moment ago, it doesn't work when you are starting out, and here's why…

You are competing with hundreds, sometimes thousands of affiliates… all of whom are promoting the same product.

However, here's the biggest reason why it doesn't work, it's because you can only capitalize on the traffic you send.

Please read that line above again until it truly sinks in…

And if you need more convincing, let me ask you a question…

Would you rather be the affiliate competing with all these other affiliates to sell my product?…

Or would you rather be the guy who has their own product for sale online who's literally doing nothing to get traffic because it's all coming from the affiliates promoting your offer for high commissions?

If you're anything like most of my students, the answer is obviously the product creator.

Now, at the time of writing this, I have almost 75,000 affiliates who have signed up to promote my products…

And that's just on JV Zoo alone.

Can you imagine if all these affiliates sent me just 1 click per day?

Now, full transparency, they don't…

Normally it's the top 5% of my affiliates who are responsible for most of the traffic, but you get the point…

It's much better to have 75,000 people working to sell your product, than it is to be one of the 75,000 competing to sell someone else's.

John Thornhill

So, let me ask you a question.

How would your business be different if you had thousands of affiliates sending you sales for your offers every day?

And, more importantly, what if I could show you how to achieve this without experience or an email list of your own?

Well, stay tuned, because later I'm going to show you how you can do exactly that.

But first...

WHY DIGITAL ASSETS ARE BEST

Now, it's kind of strange for me to think about this, but since 2004, basically 24 hours a day, 7 days a week…

I have had people buying, listening to, watching, and going through my digital products.

That's huge leverage.

Because I don't have to be there doing it anymore.

My digital products do the teaching for me, so I can have more of my time freed up to live my life.

And many of my students from around the world are following in my footsteps and using digital products to build the lives of their dreams.

But first, let me transport you back to 2003, because I want to tell you a quick story that includes a very important lesson…

At the time, I'd been trying all kinds of things to make money online, and one of the things I had some early success with was eBay.

In fact, you can look up my eBay account 'planetsms' and you'll see that I have generated over 25,000 sales and have over 17,000 feedback points.

John Thornhill

Anyway, before I had any success, I found someone selling a collection of 25,000 eBooks with resale rights on a CD rom for $50. (Remember this was back in 2003)

The CD that was sent to me dropped through my letterbox in a plain envelope and probably cost no more than $3-4 to produce and ship.

It was at that moment when this CD arrived that I remembered I had paid $50 for it, and I realised that after costs and fees the seller had probably generated about $40 - $45 profit.

Wow! Talk about easy money...

Remember that this product had resale rights so could be resold, so at first, I decided to copy it and sell the same disc at the same price and make my fortune... but there's a catch with eBay.

Other sellers can see what items you've sold and exactly how much they have sold for and when they see a seller doing well, they always copy, which meant everyone else who saw what was going on ended up doing the exact same thing and this CD saturated eBay. In the end I sold a grand total of zero CDs as others were doing it much cheaper.

However, that's when I had the brainwave that changed my life...

Instead of selling the disc and struggling to make a sale like everyone else, why not take the best eBooks from the collection and sell them individually for $1-2?

So that's exactly what I did.

I took around 200 eBooks from this collection and created some basic sales pages and listed them individually and they started to sell.

In the early days when an eBook sold I was literally manually sending people an email with a link to a ZIP file at the time. (Again, remember that this was in 2003 and it was seen as very easy work)

But over the next 6 months, I learned to automate the process and I created download pages, and built an automated delivery system, and once this was in place, I didn't have to lift a finger when a sale was made, things were going really well.

But that's not my big life changing breakthrough. My big breakthrough came when I started teaching others how I was doing it.

After all, I was selling roughly 100-150 eBooks per day and because this was eBay people could see my sales history and they knew that I was doing well, and they wanted to see how I was doing it.

So, I put together a program for $97 teaching what I knew…

John Thornhill

I included all the eBooks I was selling, I included sales page templates, download templates and delivery emails and showed exactly how to model my successful eBay business.

And virtually overnight, I went from making around $100-$150 a day, to making over $1,000 a day.

I was still working in the car plant at the time and quite often I would go to work on the production line and while I was there, I would earn a month's wages from my online business during a shift while building cars. I'm not sure if you can imagine how distracting this was, but giving up a stable job that pays well is hard to do and it took me 6 months watching this happen before I finally plucked up the courage to quit my job and go it alone.

And from 12 noon on June 3rd 2006, the day I walked out of the car plant I have been free to live my life how I choose.

So, the takeaway from this chapter is the following…

If you learn how to do anything online, whether it's list building, generating traffic, building a blog, writing content, marketing on Facebook, putting videos on YouTube, etc, etc etc…

You will usually make a lot more money teaching what you know.

And that's why I always tell my students…

If you want to generate 6 figures per year online, you simply must be selling your own products and services!

In fact, think of ANY successful marketer online, marketers such as:-

Frank Kern
Ryan Deiss
Russell Brunson
Mike Filsaime
Gary Vaynerchuk

What's the one thing they all have in common?

They all have their own products that teaches their expertise!

Don't get me wrong, I'm not saying they don't sometimes make money promoting other people's products as an affiliate.

They absolutely do.

But for the most part, that's not how they got started, and it's certainly not where the bulk of their revenue comes from.

How do I know this to be true? Simple...

Because over 80% of my revenue comes from my own digital products!

John Thornhill

Now, if you're anything like most people, you're probably thinking...

"But John, how is this possible for a beginner? I wouldn't even know where to start!"

Well, that's what we are going to cover in the next chapter...

GENERATING PRODUCT IDEAS

Make sure you check out the additional training to accompany this chapter by going to:

https://johnthornhill.com/product-ideas

The first step you need to take before you create any product of your own is to target your niche.

You want to identify a mass audience of people that are already spending money to solve a common problem.

After all, we don't want to guess whether people will buy our product, so that's why we always start by following the money.

After all, no-one wakes up and says, "I want to buy this product today!"

Instead, they're thinking about the emotional implications of their problems, decisions, and goals.

"What if I'm losing dates and respect because of my thinning hair?"

"How can I get traffic to my website?"

"What does the future look like for my family if I can't get this business off the ground?"

What if, what if, what if.

John Thornhill

Your job is to identify these desires and tap into them with your products that offer the solution.

If you do this well, your buyer will automatically trust you. Because who doesn't trust someone who "gets" them?

You see, the biggest mistake I see in people who are creating their digital products is actually a self-esteem issue...

And the mistake is thinking they don't know enough...

Or that they don't have the right credentials to create a digital product they can sell online...

In fact, when I decided to create my first product, I thought the same thing!

But here's what I learned...

I call it the 80/20 Rule.

And when you apply it, you'll quickly find that you do NOT need to be "The Expert of All Experts" on your topic.

You just need to know 20% more than 80% of the general population about that topic.

Which means if you spend just 4 to 5 hours researching a topic...

It could be a hobby, passion, or something you're interested in…

Then you can create a digital product around that topic that people will buy…

Because you now know 20% more than 80% of the general population about that topic, right?

Plus, if you can describe someone's problem better than they can…

Something I'm going to teach you how to become great at…

Then they will automatically view you as the expert and assume that you must have the solution.

So, you might not feel like an expert right now…

But let me ask you this:

What is **ONE** thing that your friends and family always come to you for advice on?

It could be anything from your knowledge of marketing and finance to your skills in education, cookery, DIY, arts and crafts…

Which means that if you've achieved a result for yourself or others…in any area of your life, then you can teach how you did it in your product.

John Thornhill

It doesn't matter how young or old you are. It doesn't matter how qualified you are.

Only that you have achieved a result with the subject you want to teach, have passion for what you do, and that you're willing to share it.

Still not convinced you've got what it takes?

Well, let me ask you another question:

What is a hobby or passion of yours that you could talk about for hours on end and never get bored of?

This doesn't have to be something you're skilled at, or even knowledgeable about yet. It just needs to be something you're interested in.

Hopefully you're already getting some ideas but if you are a bit stuck then another approach is to interview an expert.

And what I mean by this is…

You're going to find an expert in your niche and interview them…

And then turn the recordings into a digital product.

You can even have the audios transcribed and bundle them together with a written report for higher perceived value.

Or another way to approach this is to create a list of the most popular blogs in your niche...

Use a site like Quora.com, forums, or Amazon book reviews to find out what questions people in your niche are asking...

Then curate the answers from the list of popular blogs you created.

This is perfectly legal and ethical to do as long as you include (and link back to) the source of the original article somewhere in your product.

Now, the third approach (and my favourite) is to use PLR material...

Just in case you didn't know, private label rights products are a form of resale rights products that allow you take a product created by other experts and sell it as your own... and keep one hundred percent of the profits.

Now, I like to teach with examples, so let me ask you this:

Have you ever bought an item from the saver range at the grocery store?

Well, guess what!

You probably bought a private label product in the form of own brand products such as soups, biscuits, frozen foods and a whole lot more.

It's no secret that food giants produce "own-brand" versions for supermarkets…

In fact, in 2017, budget supermarket chain Aldi's own-brand Hula Hoops were proven to be the same as the real thing when a shopper found original brand packs in an Aldi multipack.

A spokeswoman for KP Snacks said: "This looks like an unfortunate error at the packaging stage which we are investigating."

She confirmed: "KP Snacks does make products for Aldi at the same site as its own Hula Hoops brand, although the products are made on different lines and to different formulations."

So, the question is…Why doesn't Aldi just manufacture the product themselves, in-house? Wouldn't they make more money that way?

Well, not always as it's often cheaper to let someone else do the hard work and let you have their finished material, and with digital PLR products quite often someone else has done the hard work of researching a profitable niche and coming up with the content that can help you create something of your own.

You can also quite often purchase audio files and software scripts with PLR rights for pennies on the dollar…

Which means the possibilities are limitless!

So basically, all you're doing with this approach is finding quality PLR material…

Using it for research purposes…

Changing the format…

Making sure the content is relevant and up to date…

And then re-branding and selling it as your own under a new name.

Simple, right?

But you might be thinking…

"This sounds great, John. But don't I need technical skills to create a digital product like this?

And my answer is always no, and we will be covering this in the next chapter…

CREATING YOUR PRODUCT

Product creation is not as hard as you think...

Long gone are the days of learning learn HTML, CSS, FTP, MySQL, and whatever other crazy technical terms you can come up with...

Which is what I had to do when I first got started...

And, believe me, I'm not tech savvy at all.

But nowadays, the wealth of tools and software at your disposal to help you build your online business have lowered the traditional barriers to entry and made it much, much easier for regular people to succeed.

Heck, these days you can get a video online in a matter of seconds with just your cell phone, back when I started it would have taken about an hour to get a video online.

And creating web pages is so much easier now with a host of page builders out there with premade templates to help you create amazing sales pages, download pages, JV pages and more. Back when I started, we literally had to learn to code in HTML and one wrong move could destroy your whole site.

So please understand what I'm saying when I tell you that you've never had it so good if you want to create your own product.

What I'm going to do now is walk you through the 3 digital product creation levels, and how to choose the RIGHT one for you.

Pay close attention, because at the end of this chapter I want you to decide how you're going to create your digital product.

Are you ready?

Okay…

Level 1 - The How-To Guide.

You create and deliver your product in the form of a simple PDF eBook. Just as I'm doing here.

You can also have your eBook read and offer the audio file as a bonus or additional upgrade offer for added value. Just as I'm doing here ☺

This is Level 1.

Now, here's what you'll need:

1. A computer.
2. Microsoft Word, Pages, or Google Docs (for writing and editing your eBook content)
3. And Audacity (if you want to offer an audio version of your eBook as bonus)

I'm a big believer in keeping it simple and with this strategy, you don't need fancy recording equipment, microphones, or anything like that. In fact, you will notice that I don't even have any images in this eBook as I will be linking to further training online if I feel that it requires more info, but of course, if you want to add images that is absolutely fine.

Now, who's a good fit for Level 1?
Well, you're a good fit for this level if this is your first time creating a digital product, and you don't feel comfortable recording your voice or appearing on-camera.

Level 2 - The Video Series.

This is where you create your product using recorded slide deck presentations.

You can also add in some over-the-shoulder, screen capture-style videos to help keep things interesting and engaging.

However, you do not need to appear on-camera at any time.

What I tend to do is record a presentation explaining a topic and then record the process using screen recording software.

For example, if I was recording a blogging guide, I may record a presentation showing how important blogging is and go into detail why you should have a blog. Then I'll record videos showing how to create a blog with WordPress and install some basic plugins.

Can you see how easy this can be with a little bit of research and planning? You could literally spend a few hours learning about blogging and how to set up a simple WordPress blog, then record the whole process and people would pay you to learn how it's done.

So, for this level, all you need is:

1. A computer.
2. PowerPoint, Keynote, or Google Slides for building your slides.
3. Screenflow (Mac) or Camtasia (Windows) to record and edit your videos.

Now, who's a good fit for Level 2?

Well, you're a good fit for this level if this is your first time creating a digital product, but you feel confident recording your voice, or you just don't like writing.

If this is the case, I would always recommend going with a video series because people love video.

Level 3 - The Simple Software Solution.

You deliver your solution in the form a WordPress Plugin.

And, before you start panicking, let me assure you:

This does not require technical skills, because you'll be hiring a coder to customize a plugin script you purchased with unlimited resale rights...

So, you don't need to know how to code or anything like that.

For this Level, you'll need:

1. A computer
2. A FREE account at CodeCanyon.net (for your plugin script)
3. And Fiverr (so you can find a coder to customize and brand your plugin for cheap)

So, who's a good fit for this level?

Well, you're a good fit for Level 3 if you have some experience creating digital products...

And you feel ready to take your authority and branding to the next level.

Now, obviously, I don't recommend you start out here...

But once you've got some early results, this is usually one of the BEST ways to scale your digital product business to the six, seven, or even eight figure level.

Now, I thought I'd mention that I have launched over 10 software products over the years and I didn't create any of them, I simply had an idea and got my programmer to make it happen.

I usually generate my software ideas by seeing something online and thinking to myself "this is rubbish" or "I can do better than that" and I draw up a plan of what I want the software to do and hand it to my programmer and she makes it happen.

Let me ask you, have you ever bought or saw something that was poor quality and had ideas to make it better? Well with the help of a programmer you can make this happen.

Heck, if you decide to go to johnthornhill.com/more and work with me I can even help you come up with ideas and then give you access to my programmer.

So, which product creation level is best for you right now?

Well, I hope that you start with Level 1, and progress through the levels with each new product you create.

But wherever you decide to start, whichever level you feel comfortable with…

"This all sounds well and good, John…

But even if I could create a digital product like this, how would I get traffic and make sales?"

John Thornhill

Well don't worry, this will be covered later in this book.

A PRODUCT IDEA YOU CAN RUN WITH RIGHT NOW

In this chapter I am going to give you a product idea that you can run with right now and within weeks you could have a product for sale teaching what I am about to show you.

This can be done by anyone regardless of experience and I guarantee it will appeal to a huge audience and is literally guaranteed to sell if done right.

First, before we go through this, let me ask you a question.

As you probably know there are literally hundreds of different free traffic methods out there. So, here's the question.

Do you think if you focussed on just one free traffic method you could get to 100 visitors per day within 21 days?

Now, when I say focussed, I mean really focussed, spending at least a few hours every single day working on nothing but your newfound traffic method?

And just in case you're struggling for traffic ideas here's a few off the top of my head.

John Thornhill

Blogging
Social Media Content
YouTube Content
Forums
SEO
Backlinks
Squeeze Pages
Twitter Posts
Infographics
Podcasting
Reviews
Interview an Expert

So, you pick one topic, and you focus on nothing but driving traffic via that topic for 21 days? Remember that you can buy products on your chosen topic and use places like The Warrior Forum for research. If you're not familiar The Warrior Forum with it's a place hundreds of thousands of marketers have visited over the years and is a great place to learn a host of Internet Marketing topics.

After a few days of research, you will be able to start implementing what you've learned. Remember that you need to focus on your newfound traffic tactic religiously for at least 14-21 days, but more importantly you need to document your progress. Listing any wins that you have and any methods that don't work.

Here's the question again...

Do you think if you focussed on just one free traffic method you could get to 100 visitors per day within 21 days?

I'm hoping that you have answered yes because I can almost guarantee that if you focus on one traffic method and nothing else for up to 21 days you will be able to get to 100 visitors per day.

And this leads me to my next question…

Do you think people would want to learn how you did it?

I'm hoping you've just had a lightbulb moment as I've literally just handed you the keys to the castle.

You see, traffic generation is one topic that never gets old as everyone wants to drive more traffic to their websites regardless of how much traffic they are currently getting, you could even ask Mark Zuckerberg if he wants to get more traffic to Facebook and I guarantee his answer would be a resounding yes.

However, a lot of marketers struggle to get any sort of traffic to their websites, usually because they don't stick with a single method long enough.

So, if you had a step-by-step guide showing how you could drive 100+ visitors per day by using a proven simple method that will only take a few weeks to implement do you think it would sell?

John Thornhill

Of course, it would.

So, go and learn a single traffic method and document the whole process and create a simple guide showing how you did it. This could be a simple PDF report or a step-by-step video series, either way it won't take long to put together.

You could even offer resale rights as an upsell to create a mini sales funnel. Or even offer some advanced traffic training as another upsell.

Once you have your product online then you'll need to create a simple sales page, JV page and download page and list it for sale. You shouldn't struggle for traffic as you could implement what you have learned and of course you will hopefully get some JVs promoting as you'll have your product launch listed in the JV networks and in your chosen marketplace.

And it really is as simple as that, now of course this whole process will take some work and it may take a little longer than 21 days to get the results desired, but if you worked at this there's no reason why you can't be launching your very own traffic guide in the next 2-3 months that has the potential to generate 6 figures long term.

However, as I've said a few times now most people won't do anything with this information as it involves actual work, but for the people who are prepared to put the work in this could be life changing.

Plus remember that I can help you do this and all you need to do is visit johnthornhill.com/more to take things further.

John Thornhill

RESEARCHING YOUR TOPIC

I know we briefly covered researching your chosen topic in a previous chapter, but now it's time to go into that in more detail.

Once you have identified a profitable niche the next thing you need to do is research your topic. When you do this, you gather all the valuable information you can find ready to compile into your chapters or modules.

Remember that when you are doing this, it's fine to look at someone else's work for research purposes, but you must never copy someone else's work, doing this could land you in serious trouble and could end your business before you've got it off the ground.

For example, if you read this book and created a book of your own on the same topic in your own words that would be fine as all the work is your own, but if you copied paragraphs from this book and pasted them into your book that would not be allowed.

The only exception to this rule is when using PLR material and I'll cover that later.

Here are some of the best places to do your research.

Forums.

Forums can be a fantastic resource and as I said earlier The Warrior Forum is an amazing place to do any sort of research in the Internet Marketing space, and no matter what topic you are looking for as long as it's Internet Marketing related you should be able to find a ton of material that will help.

When you search for your chosen keywords, you want to be looking for questions people are asking, and the problems people are having.

Then you want to be looking for the answers other people are providing. For example, if someone was asking how to get more engagement in their blog posts and you were creating a blogging guide the answers provided would help you compile a great chapter or module for your product.

I promise if you spend 2-3 hours in The Warrior Forum alone, you'll probably be able to get 50% of the research done for just about any product in the Internet Marketing space.

Blogs.

Blogs can be a fantastic resource and can help you research a ton of material. When researching other marketers' blogs one thing you want to pay attention to is the posts that have gotten the most interest. This can usually be gauged by the number of comments and shares. Obviously if you find a post in your chosen niche with a ton of comments pay particular attention to what is being discussed to see if it can help generate some ideas.

Marketplaces.

Most info products are sold via marketplaces such as JVZoo, Warrior+ and ClickBank. There are others out there but for me those are the big 3. They can also be a huge resource for research purposes and especially in finding out how other marketers are selling their offers.

For example, if I was creating a blogging guide, I'd check these marketplaces to see what's on offer and create a swipe file of the sales pages that have sold the most products. I'm going to repeat what I said earlier here, it's okay to look at another marketer's material for research purposes but never ever copy.

Also, when you check out marketplaces you can also look at …

Other Marketers Products.

When doing your research, you are going to find a few fantastic looking products in the same niche you have chosen and my advice to you is to invest in these products.

For example, if I see a marketer who has sold thousands of copies of their product in a niche I am entering, I'd want to invest in it to see the following:

Price points. I'd want to know exactly how much the offer sells for.

Upgrade offers. I'd want to know what offers are made after the initial purchase.

Content delivery. How is the content delivered?

Backend offers. Is there a high-ticket backend offer such as a webinar?

You can often learn more just be watching how other marketers sell their products than consuming their products. If you are old enough to remember Jeff Walkers Product Launch Formula what taught product launching, you could learn a lot just by watching him launch the product.

And without sounding contradictory you of course want to consume the content as you are going to learn a lot here, especially if it's a product that has sold thousands of copies and the marketer has a good reputation.

Once you have fully researched your topic and gathered all of the useful information you can it's time to start compiling your content into workable modules.

MIND MAPPING YOUR WAY TO SUCCESS

Make sure you check out the additional training to accompany this chapter by going to:

https://johnthornhill.com/mindmapping

The day I discovered Mind Mapping was the day everything changed for me as it enabled me to take an idea and brainstorm these ideas to create even more ideas that branched out as I did my research.

The general idea of Mind Mapping is to capture the thinking that goes on in your head. To do this we create 'branches' in the form of ideas and then add similar ideas to make them branch out, as we do this the process continues until we have a lot of branches. (Ideas)

For example, if I said the word 'blogging' to you what would you think?

I'm guessing you'd start to think about creating content, writing blog posts, having authority in a niche etc, and all of these could be branches.

So, let's use some form of Mind Mapping and see where it takes us.

Blogging > Builds Authority > Gains Trust > Seen as an Expert

This can branch out to.

Seen as an Expert > Research > Writing > Post useful content > Getting engagement

Which can branch out to.

Getting engagement > Encourage comments > Reward for sharing > Install sharing plugins

This is Mind Mapping in a very basic form but a matter of minutes, I have some content that could use to create numerous modules or chapters, if I spend no more than an hour doing this, I could have the outline of a full-blown online course.

You can perform Mind Mapping using just a pen and paper, but I prefer to use Mind Mapping software as it gives a more visual idea of what you are doing. There is a ton of Mind Mapping software out there, but my favourite is an app called iThoughts HD on the iPad as it means I can have my iPad close by and add ideas as I have them. You can also check out FreeMind for the Mac and PC.

Be sure to check out my Mind mapping training videos in the resources section and check out a great article on this topic here.

https://simplemind.eu/how-to-mind-map/basics/

Make sure you try this as believe me it could change everything for you and help you generate more ideas than you ever thought possible.

USING OTHER PEOPLES CONTENT FOR SPEEDY PRODUCT CREATION

I remember the first time I discovered private label rights (PLR) material and realised I could use the content as if it were my own. I am not joking here when I say I could not believe that someone else had created content and I could use it as if I had created it myself. This really was a game changing moment for me, and my head was spinning with ideas.

Reminder. Private label rights products are a form of resale rights products that allow you take a product created by other experts and sell it as your own… and keep one hundred percent of the profits.

Think about this for a moment. An expert has done most of the things I am covering in this book, they have done the niche research, created the product, in most cases created a sales page, created graphics and gave you other promotional material such as articles and ready written emails, and in some cases, they could even have created a complete sales funnel and JV page to recruit affiliates.

It really does sound too good to be true, and to a certain extent it is, as long as you use the materials you have the right way, and the thing is most people make huge mistakes when using PLR material.

John Thornhill

The main mistake I see people make is they don't change any of the content they have at their disposal, they simply slap an order button on the sales page, upload everything and expect to make a ton of sales. What you must realise is PLR vendors sell hundreds and sometimes thousands of copies of their material and this is why they do it.

When you have the same product that hundreds, and sometimes thousands of other people own you're selling the same thing as everyone else, and it doesn't take long to start to see others doing the exact same thing.

The key is to edit the content you have and make it your own.

A lot of people over-complicate this process more so than it has to be. If you want to make PLR material work for you, you need to make it your own. That's what repurposing means. It means taking the material that you've gotten, that you've got the rights to, and then customize it, add your own flair to it, change some things around, add some things, maybe create some new versions of the stuff that you've just purchased.

Let's say you have a PLR product, and 300 other people also have it. They've got the same sales page; they've all got the same graphics, the same report. A lot of people just expect to put a buy button on and expect to make sales.

Now, this page is going to get seen time and time again by different people. Yes, the Internet is fast, but it's going to happen. If you repurpose it, make it your own, then it is literally your own. You'll have a 100% unique product, so you need to be repurposing the content. When you repurpose the PLR material, you're making it personal to you, and you're differentiating yourself from other sellers.

You're not the sole buyer of PLR material unless you have a specific situation like reaching out to someone individually and asking directly if they would be willing to sell you PLR rights?

Because of this, in most cases, you will be using Private Label Rights material that other people are using too. When you repurpose it, you're making it unique. In many cases, people won't even tell the difference, because you've changed the graphics, changed the title, and even rearranged the material inside.

Before you begin to repurpose your PLR, it's important you gather all the material you have. Usually, with PLR, when you're creating your product from Private Label Rights material, it's recommended that you don't just use one source. I recommend that you use as many sources as you can. You take those sources, gather that information, and compile it into a unique creation of your own eBooks, reports, articles, and graphics, bring everything together into one collection.

John Thornhill

This is where a little bit of creativity goes a very long way. This is a part again where people will struggle because some people are lazy by nature and maybe not prepared to put the work in, but this is probably why you need to do a bit of research, you need to put some work in.

You want to gather everything so you can prepare to create the product. So, make sure that you're looking at many different sources. You also might not just be looking at the PLR material you have, you might also be looking at other marketers as well. It's okay to look at what other marketers are doing for research purposes.

The important thing is to gather as much information as possible. You want to start with a blank Google Doc or Mind Map where you can make a list of things you want to accomplish. This will just serve as a reminder that you have to find material and slides; you have to find blog posts. Then, go and look for that stuff, do searches for it all.

When you find something that interests you, whether it's a sales page of a similar product, you can copy that link and put it in that doc. When you're done with 20–30 minutes' worth of research, now you have a document containing many links and has a bunch of resources.

You've already purchased some PLR that you found, but start with this one document, and then you start compiling everything into there. Slowly, over time, it turns into what your product is going to be. Once you've gathered all your material, you can do further research.

You can plan the sales funnel. Reverse engineer the process. What's the thing that you want to sell in the back-end? What's the big-ticket product that you want to sell? You should always have some sort of webinar or something higher ticket that you're promoting. We'll talk a little bit more about that later.

When you're mapping out the PLR, when you are considering what you are going to repurpose, there are a few questions you should ask yourself. What will you use? What's the purpose? Why are you making this product? What components should you modify?

It's essential that, at the very least, you change the product's name. This is something you absolutely should do. You should do a lot more, but at the very least, that product you buy, or you got the rights to will have a name.

You need to come up with your own unique name. You want to make sure that the domain name is available when you're thinking of a new product name.

This is a standalone product with a standalone domain name so there's not much point in coming up with the name if the domain name is already taken.

So, try and make sure you can get the domain name when you come up with your product name. That's very, very important. The domain is huge because if you don't have a domain that goes with the product's name, it will be more challenging for people to remember where it is and for affiliates to know.

If the name of your product is Acme eBooks, then you should try to find acmeebook.com. In the process of renaming, don't just make a product, come up with a unique name, get graphics ordered, and later find out that domain name isn't available. Do both at the same time.

You also want to change the graphics to make the product look different, even without changing copy or anything like that. Imagine you have a banner; you've got the original product and got one with a different name and different graphics. Put them side-by-side, and they instantly look different.

If you don't know how to do this, get someone else to do it, I can help with this via:

johnthornhill.com/more.

I've seen so many products online where the person who's selling the products thinks they've created a great software box or an eBook cover, and it looks awful.

So, unless you are a pro graphic designer get a professional to do this. You can get a cover designed for $10–$20.

Remember with PLR material you may also receive the source files as well, which can make it easier. Sometimes, there's not a lot you can do with a source file, so my opinion and what I tend to do is just get the graphics created from scratch.

However, if you've got good source files, you can also do it that way. But please, unless you are proficient with Photoshop, outsource it to a professional. If I could just scream this from the rooftops, I would. Image is everything in marketing. Everything, and if you're not willing to invest a couple of bucks into redoing your graphics or making something look good, why would or should someone else invest in buying your product?

Remember that you'll never get a second chance to make a first impression, and if you're wondering, well, it's a digital product. Why do I need a cover of a box? The answer is simple; the mind thinks in pictures. Subconsciously, if your prospect can't see or picture your product in their mind's eye, it doesn't exist. So, even though it's a digital product, you should have a box covering an image of what that would look like as a book. Just as I did with this book.

John Thornhill

Reproposing Content.

You might want to take some material from one PLR product, repurpose it, and add it to another PLR product.

You might even have two or three reports on the same topic. Rate them all, and then come up with your best version of them. Make sure you're adding material and rewriting it as well.

You don't just want to copy and paste, this is because you want to make sure that when you add content, you make it as original as possible. You should always add content to PLR material and make original content.

Sometimes, you can reuse content from other products, other PLR. Adding original content does two things:

1. It forces you to read what's already there.
2. It makes your content unique.

There'll be certain areas of the PLR material that, as you're reading it, you'll think, "oh wow - this could use an extra sentence or can be expanded on a little bit more."

Maybe you can add some bullet points or highlight a specific thing that the original writer didn't do. When you're doing that, not only are you forcing yourself to improve the quality of the material. You're doing quality assurance because you're reading what was already there.

You're also customizing and putting your flair on it. Adding to the content while adding your own flair is very important. Everyone's got their own unique style of writing. You want to try and inject your personality into whatever it is you're doing, whether it be a report, a set of slides, whatever it may be. You want to make sure you're editing the content, so it's unique to you.

When you do that, the product is now 100% unique. Now, if you don't do that and you just leave the content as it is, it's something a lot of people may already have. So, make sure you add and edit as much content as possible.

Something to watch out for here is to be mindful of what you're adding and what you're editing so that you don't go off on a tangent in the wrong direction.

Remember, if you just put together a bunch of different ingredients of different recipes, you're not necessarily going to come up with a delicious tasting dish. If you're taking a piece from here, a piece from there, and also combining it without really being mindful of making sure that you're staying on topic, staying on track, and that everything flows, it will be poorly put together, and your customers will not be happy.

John Thornhill

Sometimes, the writing styles are different so you must keep an eye on that as well. Whether you are editing the content or adding material, make sure you're not just slapping a bunch of stuff together. If you do this, then all you're doing is coming up with a collage that's going to be difficult for your reader to follow. So, make sure that you're mindful of this as you're creating your content.

You may find it might be necessary to update or even remove content. We all know the Internet changes so fast and websites change from day-to-day. You can look at Facebook and see how often they change everything.

Some of the content that was maybe written a few months ago or even a few weeks ago might need to be updated. So, make sure you do that. Also, there might be a particular chapter or a specific module that's no longer relevant, so you would want to remove that. Make sure you check any links, any kind of reference made by the material you will be sharing with people. For example, if the writer referred to a particular website, you're going to want to check that website and make sure it's still up.

For example, I was going through a PLR product, and most of the material still held true to this day because a lot of it was just timeless concepts. But then, in one section of the PLR material, the writer was referring to specific websites and links. I noticed that one of the sites wasn't even around anymore.

You're going to want to make sure that you look for that kind of information that was shared in the original documents. This is just one of the many reasons why you don't want just to change the name, slap your name, and just put it back out there.

You want to go through it all, modify, add content, edit it, you might find, for example, that the original creator has linked to something and put their affiliate link. Make sure if there are any links in it and, if possible, use your own affiliate link so you get paid instead of the original creator.

Changing Format.

This is probably one of the most common things recommended that you do with your PLR content. The majority of PLR content that is out there is mostly text and you'll usually get an eBook that has PLR rights. It's still just a book that comes with the source files. You'll have either the Word doc or you'll have some sort of a text file.

Now, that text can be turned into various things. Go through that text, pick out specific sentences, turn those into bullets on a slide, and maybe a PowerPoint slide. Then, record those PowerPoint slides and turn them into videos. You're expanding the content that you have in text and turning it into slideshows. Again, there are so many different ways that you can do this, but I have to say that audio and video presentations from the text that you purchased

PLR rights to are probably one of the best things you can do.

Here is another example. You might have an eBook with 15 chapters. Take the eBook and create 15 training modules. From the training modules, you can create physical how-to videos. Now you're also opening up another door to the way that you sell it. Now, you can sell it as a recurring membership, instead of giving it all at once.

What's to stop you from maybe dripping in one of those chapters and one of those segments of content per week or month? Perhaps, instead of charging $20 for your information course or your digital product, maybe charging a $10 a month fee. You're going to end up making much more over time with the product than you would be selling it just once.

Again, every single chapter can be turned into a look-over-the-shoulder kind of a video. You can quickly go through the prewritten text and pick out the parts you could talk on. You could go through a chapter and pick up five things that you know you could expand on and turn those into talking points in a video.

You can then take the entire chapter and make five videos out of that. There are just so many different combinations that are truly endless. It only comes down to how you want to do it. It's not just about the bullets and slides, either. Suppose the topic, for example, was maybe explaining a process. Why not actually turn your webcam or your screen capture on, go to the website, and even create a video showing an over-the-shoulder type of presentation of how to do the process you were talking about in the content.

When you do a presentation about something you're already familiar with, maybe you just need 5–10 words or 5–15 words for a bullet. When you see those bullets, you can talk for two or three minutes about each bullet. You can take some content in a report, take the key points, and then put one or two lines for the bullet, prompting you to talk about that particular segment.

You could be looking at a report while recording your voice, using the bullet points you're looking at, as a prompt, so you know what to talk about. If you think about it, this makes for a much more engaging video because who wants to sit there and listen to someone read exactly what's on the screen?

It's one of the reasons that I use what I call the 5-5-5 method which is five bullets and five slides that takes five minutes per slide to record.

If I can talk for five minutes, basically, one minute on each one of these bullets, I'm going to end up with a 25-minute video.

The reality is you can usually talk for two minutes. So, you're going to end up with a video that's going to be anywhere from 45–50 minutes. That can end up being quite a bit of text when it's turned into a transcription.

When you consider that now, you took the PLR material, you turned it into bullets that just served as talking points, and you talk for two minutes.

You're now creating new material when you're talking on those bullet points. Next, get it all transcribed, then you can take that and include it as part of your PLR product. It just expands the whole thing. It makes it so much more valuable, and it really is giving that wow factor to it.

You can also create PDF content from audio and video; it works both ways.

We just talked about taking text and creating videos, how-to videos, slide videos, or using bullet points. But you could do the other way around as well. If you have audio or video, you can turn that into a PDF. You want to be looking at ways to repurpose the content as much as possible.

Remember! You want to aim to create a 100% unique product. If you have both products side by side, the average person looking would not know because if it's 100% unique, it's 100% unique to you, you have something no one else has. That's when you can charge a premium. Having a 100% unique product, meaning...you took your ideas, your own format, and some basic concepts from the PLR, but now it's 100% unique.

WRITING YOUR SALES PAGE

Make sure you check out the additional training to accompany this chapter by going to:

https://johnthornhill.com/your-sales-page

Most people think they need an email list of their own to have a successful launch. They think launches are reserved only for big-name marketing gurus with their huge email lists, million-dollar advertising budgets, and an entire team behind them…

And nothing could be further from the truth!

The truth is Affiliates and JV partners are always on the lookout for quality products to promote. Which means that if you create a good product you can leverage other people's audiences to launch it, while building your own list of buyers at the same time!

See, when it comes down to it, there are only two things that affiliates look for.

The first is a quality product. So, make sure your product is the best it can be.

The second most important thing potential affiliates look for, by far, is your sales page. I mean, think about it…

Affiliates want to make money, right?

So, if they can see your sales page is likely to convert, they're more likely to want to promote you because they know they're going to make more money.

So, with that in mind let me walk you through the three elements you must include on your sales page to maximize sales and conversions and make your launch as attractive as possible to potential affiliates and JV partners.

Element #1 is Your Headline.

Did you know that most jurors at a trial make their minds up about the guilt of a defendant within the opening arguments of a trial? Well, that's the headline. The rest of the trial is just to confirm their initial belief.

The fact is, whether you like it or not, people are going to make up their mind about your product in a split second and 90% of people make the decision to leave in less than 10 seconds!

This is a quote from David Ogilvy, one of the founding fathers of modern advertising. He said that, on average, five times as many people read the headline as the body copy.

When you've written your headline, you've already spent eighty cents out of your advertising dollar.

Taking that into account, your headline's job is NOT to sell, but simply to get people to read further. But how?

Well, the first thing you want to do is call out to your audience in your headline, so they know immediately they are on the right page.

Don't be afraid to be specific here!

For example, if your product was in the dog training niche, you might put "Attention: Frustrated Puppy Owners!" at the top of your sales page.

Sometimes this can feel a little unnecessary, but you see it all the time, particularly from top direct marketers.

The next thing you want to do is grab their attention with a big, bold promise that tells them exactly what you are going to teach them.

And you also want to use numbers to back up your promise and make it more specific and believable.

For example, here's the headline for my product Simple Traffic Solutions.

It reads, "BANNED: Ex-Factory Worker Gets Slapped By Google... Only To Discover The Ultimate FREE Traffic Source That Brings In Up To 16,364 Targeted Visitors Per Day!"

Now, let me ask you a question:

If you were looking for a way to generate more traffic to your website, and you've tried and failed with paid traffic in the past, or are afraid to try…

Could you read this headline and not want to continue reading?

You'd have no choice but to keep reading.

Why?

Because this promise, this benefit speaks directly to the end result they want to achieve. Better yet, it's specific and believable, because we've got that 16,364 number in there, and we've also got the curiosity factor through the use of the word "BANNED".

Which creates an "open loop," and forces people to read on to figure out what I did to get myself banned.

Element #2 is Your Story.

People love stories.

That's why before and after pictures work so well in the weight loss niche. They tell a story.

But the key here is that when you're telling your story, you can't make it all about you. You have to tell a story that will resonate with them…

John Thornhill

To do this, you want to tell a story about a problem, struggle, or challenge that you experienced in the past. In doing so, you want to identify with their struggles before you explain how your solution helped you overcome adversity.

Remember, the aim of your story is not to make you look like the hero. Instead, you want people nodding along, thinking "Wow! This person is just like me." You want what you are saying to resonate with them.

Because here's the thing:

When you can describe someone's problem better than they can, they automatically assume that you know how to solve it and trust you more.

For example…

In my sales page for Simple Traffic Solutions, I tell a story about my struggles with paid traffic.

I talk about how my Google AdWords account got shut down with no explanation…

I talk about how I turned to Facebook and how, after months of trial and error just trying to get to the grips with the platform, and months of trial and error struggling to get my ads approved. I finally started to see some results before the EXACT same thing happened there, too…

And then I talk about how I tried SEO, and basically hit a brick wall there, as well.

Now!

Do you notice how, when I'm telling my story, I'm also eliminating other solutions in the marketplace they might be considering?

If anyone in my target market was considering trying Google or Facebook ads before they stumbled upon this page, there's a good chance they'll be having second thoughts now!

And that's what primes them for…

Element #3, which is Your Irresistible Offer.

Now, this is the part some people struggle with, because they believe that selling is unethical in some way, but of you believe in what you're selling, which you will if you work with me to create your product…

If you know your product solves a problem for people, which IT will, then I want you to think about Your Irresistible Offer as the next logical step.

Okay, so once you've introduced your product, I want you to have a section of your sales page that tells them everything they get and really spell it out and let them know what they're going to be paying for.

So many people skim through a sales page, that they don't know what they're going to be paying for at the end! And that's where you want to slow it down, because the people who are paying attention are the people who are thinking about buying.

Make sure they understand what you are selling with bullet points.

And you want your bullets to express a clear benefit and promise to the reader. Here's what I mean by that:

People want to buy an outcome, not a product.

No one wants to buy a weight loss guide, they want the sexy body they get as a result.

So, try to think about that when you're creating your bullets and don't just tell them what they get, but also what they'll be able to do with what they get…

For example, with Simple Traffic Solutions they get 20 powerful traffic modules…

What can they do with it? Generate all the free traffic they can handle.

They get the Simple Traffic Solutions report…

What can they do with it? Generate thousands of visitors per day to their websites.

These bullet points can be VERY compelling, and you can NEVER have too many of them…

In fact, I've lost count of the number of people who've emailed me after buying one of my products, telling me that it was one bullet in particular that tipped them over the edge.

So, let me ask you:

What could you stop doing in your life if you had a 5 or 6 figure launch?

Could you stop worrying about money?

Could you stop relying on others for your job or livelihood?

Could you stop worrying about the economy, because you know you have an asset that can you make you money on demand, no matter what's going on in the outside world?

Well, as you think about that, let's move on.

DELIVERING YOUR PRODUCT

Make sure you check out the additional training to accompany this chapter by going to:

https://johnthornhill.com/your-members-area

Once your product is complete you need to get it ready to deliver to your customers, and the best way to do this is to simply send your customers to a page where they can access what they have purchased from you.

While there are many ways to deliver your product by far the best way is to create a membership site and give your customers access via a login page. If set up right not only will this protect your content, but it will also generate a lot of extra revenue for you.

Now before you go running to the hills thinking that creating a member's area is an impossible task let me tell you it is very easy to do with the tools we have at our disposal. I use a membership script called Wishlist and you probably noticed when you purchased this book the delivery process was flawless.

Let's look at how you can generate extra revenue from your membership site, and I want to start by saying something that you may struggle to grasp and it's this…

If you do things right, it's not unusual to generate more revenue from your members area than you generate from your launch.

This is why you see some marketers offer 100% commissions on their products and sometimes even offer 100% commission on their whole funnel. This is because they know that their backend operation that starts with someone becoming a member of one of their websites will generate more revenue than the sale of the product the customer bought.

There's every chance you bought this book because an affiliate sent you here. What you may not know is I pay my affiliates 100% commission of all the products you saw when you when though my sales process when you bought this book.

I do this because I want to make my offer as attractive as possible for affiliates to promote and the more attractive my offer is the more affiliates will send me traffic.

"But John, how the heck are you making money?"

Well. Apart from having affiliate links and upgrade offers inside my members area I know a percentage of people who read this book will resonate with what I have had to say and go to johnthornhill.com/more to start working with me. Even if only 1% of the people who buy this book end up working with me, I'll be in profit.

John Thornhill

"That's easy for you John but I don't have any high ticket offers"

That's fine, you simply find something high ticket that is congruent with your main offer and promote it as an affiliate.

For example, you might make 200 sales on your frontend product that sells for $10, which would turn into $2000. If that's all you are doing, all you are going to make is $1000 if you give affiliates 50% commissions which is the standard rate.

But, if you gave away that $2,000 to affiliates by offering 100% commissions, and you added just 10% of those people into a backend webinar, and you made only two sales at $2000 and earned $1000 in commissions on each sale then you'd have made $1000 more than you would have done the entire launch.

However, I guarantee that if you offer 100% commissions you would make more sales on your frontend product than offering the standard 50%. Meaning you may make 1000 sales or more on the frontend instead of 200 sales, and if we use the same maths that would be 5x more sales, so you'd make 10 backend sales at $1000 each.

Of course, the key here is to keep sales coming in daily and have a constant stream of new customers coming into your members area, thus generating high ticket sales on complete autopilot.

Another way to generate extra revenue is inside your members area. Remember that people need to login to access your content, and this is a very powerful piece of virtual real estate. So, make sure you have affiliate links pointing to any products or services you recommend. Please watch the corresponding video that goes with this chapter to learn more.

RECRUITING JV PARTNERS

Make sure you check out the additional training to accompany this chapter by going to:

https://johnthornhill.com/jv-recruitment

Attracting quality affiliates so they will promote your product is the key to having a successful launch.

First, you want to get some metrics. If you can drive some traffic yourself, you should work out the EPCs, which stands for earnings per click. The higher your EPC is, the more affiliates you will attract.

You want to be shooting for well over $1 on average. These days, it seems like affiliates want to see $4, $5, $6, or $7 EPCs. Your job should be to get those EPCs up; then you've got more chances of attracting affiliates.

If you're offering 50% on the frontend and your EPC is $1.50, by offering 100% now, your EPCs have instantly doubled to $3. That's a figure that will attract the big affiliates.

Affiliates can now look at that number and predict how much money they're going to make because they know how many clicks they can send with their list.

Focusing on the metrics is essential when you're going to attract quality affiliates to promote.

Create sales copy that converts.

This would be a separate book or a separate presentation completely, but you need to learn this. If you search for "how to write a good copy," you're going to get a ton of excellent stuff, plus remember I show you the basics in the video that accompanies chapter 14.

Sales page templates that come with most pages builders these days make it a lot easier because you can create good looking pages. That's almost as important as the words on your screen because if your page doesn't look good, people are going to bail before they've even read anything.

But you also need to learn to write copy and as I said earlier it involves telling the reader a story. So, you need to take the reader on a journey as they scroll down your page.

Affiliates can also spot bad copy a mile away. If I'm looking at a product to promote, the first thing I check is the way the page looks. If it looks like it's been thrown together with bad graphics, wrong wording, I walk away and don't even consider it. I want to promote a good product, so the product has to be good.

Next, I want to make sure I'm going to get a decent commission if I decide to push hard for this offer. The sales copy is going to play a huge part in this. If you're looking at a sales page that looks horrible as a potential affiliate, it's a good sign of what can be expected for the product itself. If the person doesn't care about their sales page's quality, how do you think they feel about the product's quality once they've gotten the money?

Be very mindful of putting time and effort into your sales copy and your sales page because it must convert. But don't freak out about this if you're just starting. This is a learned skill. This isn't a gift from God that you're born with, or you're not. This is something that you learn as time goes on.

There are specific templates that you can use as a starting point. There's lots of training material out there to tweak and perfect your technique. But eventually, you're going to get the groove. You're going to get the things that work for your audience and the things that don't work for your audience. You're going to become better and better with each digital information product that you offer.

Your JV Page.

Your JV page is just as important as your sales page because it's "selling" your product to affiliates.

As we said earlier, affiliates are generally lazy by nature and of course, the first thing you want is a great looking page. But then, you want to make sure you give your JVs all the information they need.

How much commission can they earn?
How much can they earn if a customer buys through the whole funnel?

You might be able to say something along the lines of "you can earn up to $246 per customer." You need to tell people the commissions they're going to receive. And of course, the information about what your product delivers. They will all need email copy and all of the graphics.

Yu may also want to include information about how to get a review copy of your product as well. Also, you want to put an opt-in form in there, but do not force the JV to opt in to promote. You simply want to give them an option to keep updated with your launch.

You need all of the information such as the start date, the end date, and the start time. What happens at the end? Is the product going to go up in price?

So many JVs fail to give people that information. If the information is there, it makes it so much easier for affiliates and JV partners. Give the affiliates all of the information they need. Remember, each affiliate could get you 100 customers or more.

It almost makes more sense for you to put even more effort into the creation of your JV page than you did your sales page. This is a skill that many people brush off. They spend all their time creating their product, and then when it comes to the recruitment of affiliates and the driving of traffic, they just brush it off.

Leading up to your launch, you need to be around. Whatever communication platform you're using, whether it be Messenger, Skype, etc. you need to add those details on your JV page. Let people know how they can reach out to you.

A JV may have a specific question, and it could be a make-or-break question for them. If you don't answer that question in a timely manner, especially if you're currently live and you've got someone who's waiting to promote, then you're going to lose that JV potentially.

Finally, you want to educate your affiliates. If you've learned something that can help an affiliate to get more sales, you need to tell them.

If I see a particular affiliate doing well on one of my launches, I find out what they're doing, and I'll tell all the other affiliates. Maybe they're using a bonus, or perhaps they're doing something specific.

If I find a specific email that has converted well for me, I will include it in my JV emails. I might tell my JVs, "this email got me a 37% conversion. Here it is, use this email."

Anything you can do leading up to the launch, especially where you can educate affiliates, tell them they need to mail often. Tell them there's a bonus template you've got available. Tell them to be ready when you go live. Just make sure you've got all the information they need and educate them as much as you possibly can.

For the smaller affiliates, who drive only 10, 20 sales, what if you can double the number of their sales just by educating and giving them good stuff?

Doing this will help them get more sales, and obviously, that's going to help you get more sales. It will help you tremendously by giving your best selling tips to the people selling for you.

Educate your affiliates. It just makes a whole lot of sense. Remember that it's not just about them promoting this product. It's about them being so delighted with the results that they received promoting your product.

Being enamoured by the fact you gave them 100% commission and excellent customer service. The fact that you were there making yourself available, they will want to promote for you repeatedly, not just this product, but your next one and the one after that.

Never forget that affiliates are the key to your success. It's a part of the process you have to consider when creating a digital information product.

John Thornhill

Remember, the more money your affiliates make, the more money you make. It's as simple as that.

Give your affiliates most of the commissions, because if you've got the right setup on the backend, you can afford to do this. When you have launches happening consecutively, affiliates will remember a profitable promo. They remember a good campaign. If that's one of your products, the next time you're launching, they will be there for you.

Remember that you should also build relationships with affiliates, and it is a long-term process. Over time, you're going to build relationships with certain marketers where you know they've got your back. Where they also know they will promote you. It works both ways as well.

You don't want to be one of these marketers who disappears when you've got nothing going on, no launches in your pipeline. We see this happen often. I might message a certain JV or a potential promotion and get no response back, but then six weeks later, when they have a launch going on, guess what? They come back. You don't want to be like that. Don't be one of these guys who just disappear and then suddenly comes out of the woodwork when you've got a launch going on. It's all about relationship building.

"People don't buy what you do; they buy why you do it."
- Simon Sinek – Author & Speaker

LAUNCHING YOUR PRODUCT

Make sure you check out the additional training to accompany this chapter by going to:

https://johnthornhill.com/launching

If you are thinking about selling digital products online, then you want to get as many affiliates as possible on board. The main reason is that our products are digital in nature, and due to this, we can offer handsome commissions that are not possible when we sell physical products. This gives the digital marketer a huge advantage over a brick and mortar business.

There are also literally thousands of experienced affiliates out there who can drive endless amounts of traffic. There are a lot of things you can do to attract affiliates, but by far the best way to bring your product to the online world is to have a Product Launch and to let as many affiliates know about this as possible.

It is important to understand that product launches can be unpredictable, and unfortunately, there are many things that can and do go wrong.

For a launch to go well, you need all to make sure you have everything ready, so I have compiled this checklist for you to help you plan your launch.

Pre-Launch Checklists

Ideally, Begin This Process at Least 6 Weeks Before Launch

1. Test Funnel/no thanks links and secure member access.

2. Test autoresponder integration.

3. Check Favicons and Social Media sharing images are correct.

4. Check sales page titles and descriptions are correct.

5. Create and deploy coming soon page.

6. Create Facebook wall and Facebook Group header images.

7. Set launch date and announce on JV networks - Muncheye / Warrior JV / Launch RR / Product Launch Calendar / JV Notify Pro. (See list at bottom of this report)

8. Add a countdown timer to your JV page counting down to launch.

9. Make a top 30 JV Head-hunter list. (Personally, contact this list daily and aim to get 1 per day to commit)

John Thornhill

10. Ask your friends and affiliates to mail their JVs for you.

11. Mail affiliate list and make public announcements on personal wall and JV groups - 4-6 weeks ahead.

30 Days Before Launch.

1. Contact potential affiliates with product brief and launch date.

2. Purchase JV Solo Ads from other marketers and Facebook groups.

3. Create a 'Buzz Spreadsheet' with 30 valuable items to share (Video's / Posts / Memes / Lessons)

4. Post valuable info from spreadsheet daily in every group you belong to. (STAY RELEVANT)

5. Post and Tweet every day about your launch prep progress and give them teasers.

2 Weeks Before Launch.

1. Contact affiliates again and offer product access. Illustrate the funnel and explain the playout process.

2. Mail your own affiliates daily from this point.

3. Automatically give top JVs Access to your product.

4. Give JVs contact methods to reach you.

1 Week Before Launch.

1. Contact affiliates again checking they have what they need.

2. Advise Merchant Processors of upcoming increase in sales. (We hope)

3. Setup domain monitoring service. (Ask your host)

4. Fine tune checkout pages and shrink site images and add support contact details, privacy policy, etc.

5. Contact JVs again with final launch schedule/pricing schedule.

6. Set up headline and video split tests.

7. Set up back end members area offers.

8. Post on JV groups 3,2,1 days before launch.

9. Mail your JV List twice per day 3,2,1 days before launch.

10. Run final checks on sales material.

11. Prepare and schedule your own promotional emails.

12. Insert a Leader Board Placeholder.

John Thornhill

During Launch.

1. Monitor sales pages and make sure they are loading OK and fast.

2. Run split test in the first few hours and during high traffic.

3. Mail affiliates a few hours after you go live to keep them updated.

4. Announce early stats in Facebook groups and wall.

5. Run retargeting ads to customer audience.

6. Make daily affiliate progress announcements - Always include one swipe email that they can 'mail now'.

7. Monitor support desk and disputes.

8. Remember to mail your own list at least once per day.

9. Let staff handle product and support issues - YOUR ONLY CONCERN AT THIS STAGE IS JV'S AND CONVERSIONS.

10. Within 24 hours compare list of JVs who've promoted to those that committed and contact those who haven't mailed.

11. Keep recruiting during launch week.

12. Always be on Facebook chat, Skype, etc.

13. Keep recruiting, don't stop.

14. Keep JVs updated daily with stats and leader board updates throughout the launch via email, messenger, Skype, Facebook, etc.

After Launch.

1. After launch pay the prizes straight away. (Get tax details first)

2. Record a thank you video for JVs. use their names and compliment their traffic power.

3. Post a thank you image on Facebook.

4. Make your JV page evergreen and remove any reverence to dates, etc. Also add launch stats to recruit even more JVs going forward.

5. Contact JVs who haven't promoted and set up private promos.

6. Take a break, you've earned it!!

As you can see, launching products is a long process, full of labour, risks and obstacles but the payoff can be huge if you get it right.

John Thornhill

Most people make their biggest or most costly mistakes during the planning and pre-launch stages, so refer to this checklist as much as you need to and always have it to hand whenever you launch.

MARKETING TO YOUR NEW CUSTOMERS THE RIGHT WAY

Make sure you check out the additional training to accompany this chapter by going to:

https://johnthornhill.com/marketing

There's one thing I haven't mentioned in this book yet and it's probably the most important thing of all and that's building a mailing list. However, I'm not talking about building just any mailing list, I'm talking about building a customer mailing list.

In my opinion 1 customer is worth about 50 freebie seekers, as a customer has already spent money with you. This means they are more likely to invest in you again and again as long as you provide a good service. And when you launch your product, you will have customers in abundance and be able to mail these customers with other offers.

However, there's more to this than just sending out emails to customers and that's what I want to cover in this chapter, but before I do that there's a couple of things I want to mention first.

If it was all gone tomorrow…

You could take away everything in my business but as long as I still had my mailing list, I'd be okay. This is because if I needed to rebuild my business from scratch, I could let my subscribers know about this and keep them as customers. I'd also be able to let them know about other products and services as an affiliate to keep revenue coming in.

If you need more convincing about how important building a mailing list is then let me ask you a question.

How did you get here?

What I mean by that is how are you here reading this book right now? My guess is you received an email from myself or one of my affiliates. If that's the case, then I don't know how much more convincing you need that building a mailing list is the most important thing you need to be doing.

Anyway, let's get back to how you monetize your mailing list...

So, lets imagine you've had a successful product launch and you've got 2000 brand new customers on your mailing list.

First, you need to make sure you treat these newfound customers like royalty. This means offering outstanding service and support and overdelivering in every aspect to provide a truly outstanding customer experience.

Second, the worst thing you can do is not mail your new customers. If you are on an of my mailing lists, you'll know I mail at least once per day and often more. Do not make the mistake of thinking if you email your subscribers every day that they will unsubscribe.

This was a hard lesson for me as for years I would only mail 2-3 times per week, and then one day I decided to email more often and guess what happened?

My opens increased and my revenue tripled.

The thing is if you provide value then it's fine to email your subscribers often. So instead of thinking you've got a 2000 person cash cow from your successful launch you should be thinking how you can help these people, and if you think like this then everything will be fine.

This means always review anything you promote and don't promote rubbish products, offer bonuses, and seek out discounts for your subscribers. Basically, look after them and they will look after you.

Remember, the people you email are real, and they are at the other end of the email sat on their computer clicking a link and listening to what you have to tell them. So, make sure you genuinely have their interests at heart.

Do this and get 5000 customers on your mailing list and you'll never have to worry about money again.

John Thornhill

This is a topic that I want to go into in more detail about, so I urge you to watch the 1-hour live session that I held with Randy Smith that covers email marketing in a lot more detail. The link is at the beginning of this chapter.

THE POWER OF AUTOMATION

I want you to remember what happened when you purchased this book.

First, you probably received an email from myself or one of my affiliates and you visited the sales page and you decided to invest. From there you will have made your payment and possibly invested in some upgrades, after making your payment you would have been automatically taken to my members area where you got access everything you purchased and now you are here reading this book.

Over the coming days I will send you emails that will offer advice about creating your own product and ultimately, I will offer you the chance to join my coaching program and work with me one on one to make creating your product a reality.

The thing is, I don't have to lift a finger to make any of this happen.

Everything has been set up in advance and I just need to get traffic to my sales page and the rest will take care of itself. Over time I will sell thousands of copies of this book and in turn this will bring many people into my $2000 coaching program, and I won't have to do anything to make this happen as it's all been done in advance.

And it's not just this book that runs on 100% autopilot 24 hours per day. Have a look at

John Thornhill

https://webinarwithjohn.com/trillion-dollar-opportunity and sign up for the webinar, once you sign up, you'll be able to attend a presentation that runs every 15 minutes. Once you've attended, I'll send you a link to the replay that includes real time scarcity including a countdown timer, if you don't invest from the replay I'll make you a trial offer and if you eventually decide to join the offer that I make I'll deliver it automatically to you and you'll be able to consume the material anytime from anywhere in the world.

Remember that when you create a digital asset you only have to do it once and there's no limit to the number of units you can sell. You can create this product for literally zero cost and once created everything runs on autopilot.

This is the world we are living in right now and if you to be a part of it with my help go to:

johnthornhill.com/more

And let's start working together.

6 FIGURES AND BEYOND

We are approaching the end of this book and I hope you've enjoyed the time we have spent together. Remember that to get the most from what I have to offer to watch the additional videos that accompany many of the chapters.

I guess this is the part where everyone is expecting me to come up with an amazing offer and tell you that I've left out the most important step, and you can't succeed without it.

Well, if you've learned anything from reading this far, it should be that I'm not the typical marketer that uses hype or clickbait style tactics to sell my products and services, and if you do join me on one of my programs, you too will learn that there is no need for such methods.

I genuinely believe I've shared enough information that if followed step by step, along with the bonus video training and other materials that anyone can do this and start to make money online from their own Digital Assets!

My program simply offers more of myself and my teams time, specific answers and guidance to any challenges along the way, and a complete step by step series of videos to follow along with.

John Thornhill

When you add to that, regular training webinars, an interactive group of others on a similar path, and finally, our One on One time! Cumulating in a thorough check, that everything you have is correctly set up and ready to make you money and build your own customer list...

The only obstacle left in your way, would be getting those initial affiliates onboard to send you their traffic and that is the final piece of the puzzle my students appreciate the most.

If you join my program and with my help create a product of your own I will help recruit affiliates for you, AND, because I have helped with the whole process you followed, I know your product will be of sufficiently high quality, that I ALSO GUARANTEE to fully promote it to my own 100K customers.

Which, frankly, guarantees that you cannot fail if you are a member of my partnership to success program.

How quickly you succeed I guess, would depend on how quickly my team and I can answer any questions you may still have, and how soon you can get started with us.

So, if you're at that stage right now, go to:

johnthornhill.com/more

And select an option.

Re-watch my webinar, click to join me, check what other members have had to say, (some even share their incomes since working with me), or book a call to get those questions answered.

And hey, even if you chose to go it alone, I wish you the very best of success and I can still help you so do reach out via the link above if you have any questions.

With everything I have provided for you, you now have a plan to follow that has worked for me the last 20 years and is getting more and more popular as more and more people are coming online to learn new things. And it's up to us to provide what they are looking for and become rich doing so...

Until we speak again...

John Thornhill

P.S. Remember to go to:

johnthornhill.com/more

Whether it's for a quick strategy call, to answer any questions or to enquire about working with me.

Whatever you decide, good luck!

John Thornhill

www.ingramcontent.com/pod-product-compliance
Lightning Source LLC
Chambersburg PA
CBHW060147200526
45165CB00023B/971